Salt Modern Poets: No. 1
Barraclough, Kennard, McCabe

SIMON BARRACLOUGH was born and raised in Huddersfield, West Yorkshire and now lives in London. He won the poetry section of the London Writers' Competition in 2000 and his work has appeared in *Poetry Review, The Manhattan Review, Time Out, Magma* and the anthologies *In the Criminal's Cabinet, Unfold* and *Ask for It by Name*.

LUKE KENNARD is a poet, critic, dramatist and pugilist. He is compassionate, but prone to anxiety and bleak introspection. Many have called him polite and quite funny, but add that he suffers from a tendency towards constant nervous laughter and an apparently involuntary rictus of disdain. His poetry and criticism have appeared in *Stride Magazine, Sentence, Echo:Location, The Tall Lighthouse Review, Reactions 4, Orbis, 14 Magazine, The Flying Post, Exultations & Difficulties*. He won an Eric Gregory Award in 2005 and was shortlisted for Best Collection in the 2007 Forward Poetry Prizes. He is quite tall.

CHRIS MCCABE was born in Liverpool in 1977. His poetry has featured in a number of magazines including *Magma* and *Poetry Review*. His first collection *The Hutton Inquiry* was published in 2005. He has discussed and read his poetry on BBC World Service, featured a poem on the Oxfam CD *Lifelines* and performs his work regularly. He currently works as Joint Librarian of The Poetry Library and lives in Dagenham with his wife and son.

Also by the poets

SIMON BARRACLOUGH
Los Alamos Mon Amour (Salt 2008)

LUKE KENNARD
The Solex Brothers (Redux) (Salt 2007)
The Harbour Beyond the Movie (Salt 2007)
The Migraine Hotel (Salt 2009)

CHRIS MCCABE
The Hutton Inquiry (Salt 2005)
Zeppelins (Salt 2008)

Salt Modern Poets: No. 1

Introductions to Contemporary Poetry

SIMON BARRACLOUGH
LUKE KENNARD
CHRIS MCCABE

SALT

CAMBRIDGE

PUBLISHED BY SALT PUBLISHING
14a High Street, Fulbourn, Cambridge CB21 5DH United Kingdom

Individual poems © Simon Barraclough, Luke Kennard, Chris McCabe, 2010
Selection © Salt Publishing, 2010

The rights of Simon Barraclough, Luke Kennard and Chris McCabe
to be identified as the authors of this work has been asserted by them
in accordance with Section 77 of the Copyright, Designs and Patents Act 1988.

Salt Publishing 2010

Printed and bound in the United Kingdom by Lightning Source UK Ltd

Typeset in Swift 9.5 / 13

ISBN 978 1 84471 813 9 paperback

1 3 5 7 9 8 6 4 2

Contents

Simon Barraclough

Los Alamos Mon Amour

The second before and the eternity after
the smile that split the horizon from ear to ear,
the kiss that scorched the desert dunes to glass
and sealed the sun in its frozen amber.

Eyelids are gone, along with memories
of times when the without could be withheld
from the within; when atoms kept their sanctity
and matter meant. Should I have ducked and covered?

Instead of watching oases leap into steam,
matchwood ranches blown out like flames,
and listening to livestock scream and char
in test pens on the rim of the blast.

I might have painted myself white, or built a fallout room
full of cans and bottled water but it's clear
you'd have passed between cracks, under doors,
through keyholes and down the steps to my cellar

to set me wrapping and tagging my dead.
So I must be happy your cells have been flung through mine
and your fingers are plaiting my DNA;
my chromosomes whisper *you're here to stay.*

Saturn on Seventh

I've been giving the miraculous a whirl
but what have I got? A stomach crammed

with cheap chimichanga, a shoulder-check
from Christian Slater and, though I don't know it yet,

a cloned credit card number. The Empire State
is a popsicle dipped in its Christmas reds

and greens. "Let's eat and drink ourselves
into hospital." The waitress only just

brought you round with ice-water fingers
on the cubicle floor between courses

and flaming, straw-melting cucarachas.
We came to celebrate this town

but dragging ourselves up Seventh Ave.
back to the peeling *Pennsylvania* room,

we sway wasted and weary past
stacks of Japanese *Playboys*, Brazilian

Vogues, battlements of L. Ron Hubbard
remainders, a trestle table over-stacked

with cheaply-stitched-together baseball caps:
all the naff globalised tat we've come

to expect from the greatest city on earth.
And then this charcoal-on-cardboard sign,

See Saturn for a dollar, and the giggling line
of clubbers where a homeless astronomer

has angled a prized and battered telescope
at a quarter of the sky to the right

of the Chrysler Building, which tonight
looks like it might have been piloted here

by Buster Crabbe. I toss a dollar in his cap
expecting nothing but empty night,

rest my brow against the rubber cup,
sealing out the street-level light

and there, in a black starless spotlight:
Saturn, as fat as a two pound coin,

fluxing with my pulse conducted through
the sensitive instrument, tilts its tipsy

rings towards Manhattan. I don't want to leave
its impeccable silence but you've paid

your money too and I step aside.
A random reveller asks me, "Did you see it?

Is it real?" and "Was it in colour?"
You take your fill and turn away, smiling.

We continue up the hill in silence,
our minds in parallel universes.

The Open Road

What if colour film came first
and all these searing sunsets, curly copper mops,
pink-fringed parasols and gaudy frocks
were so much *blah* to an eye that thirsts

to watch an ashen rose unfurl,
see the charcoal sheen of a peacock's tail,
a seascape rolling in drab grayscale,
dun smudges on the cheeks of girls;

dancing flames of heatless brume,
rockets spraying asterisks of chalk,
greybells blooming on pallid stalks,
the world's flags starred and striped with gloom?

We wouldn't dress our hearts in motley threads
and fix the world in greens and reds,
projecting all the loves we said
we'd never leave but left for dead,

and might not glimpse the widening seam
between the separating reds and greens
of everything we'd thought we'd seen
on our memory's monitor or silver screen.

Contacts

Jolts awake in the early hours,
eyelids crisp as courgette flowers,
turns towards the bedside blur
and sees the clock unusually clear.
4.50 a.m. with his contact lenses
Epoxied fast to his corneas.
Feet arch on tile as he peels back the lids
and pads at an iris with fingertip
but fails to find the lip between
the contact lens and all he's seen.
He's never known them so dried on,
must be the wine, the parching sun,
unless he's nudged them round the back:
two jellyfish in the lightless black.
Unfolds a hotel razor blade
from its envelope but he's not that brave
or desperate yet. Resumes the pincer
of thumbnail and index finger
and snags at last the stubborn seal,
with focused effort starts to peel
first one lens off and then the other
and lays them on a small hand mirror.
Unscrews their double-siloed case
to find them waiting in their place.
And on the mirror, torn asunder:
asquint Picasso, boss-eyed flounder.

Pike

Teriyaki tigering the golden
deep-fried flesh and a flask of hot sake
fuming like a factory chimney.

This china smoke stack takes me back
to failing mills and Warcar Reservoir:
the stagnant pond that used to juice them

before profit migrated East to the land
of synthetics, cheap worsted, cheaper labour.
The summer of *Jaws* and tucked-up legs,

invented verrucas, sliding Sunday nights
down the gullet of the weekend bath:
feeling like Quint kicking at teeth, puking blood.

Pike were our local great whites but we had
no pike nets, pike repellent, strychnine jabs,
no police chief or ichthyologist.

We had hunks of drystone wall, giant bobbins,
window gaffs, rafts of unhinged doors,
to protect us from the monstrous fish

that Ted Hughes himself might have reared
and delivered overnight on the back
of a flat-bed lorry.

We knew the tale of the kid who dived
onto a rusting Cortina,
swam to the cobbles and bound up

his intestines in a pinkening towel
and almost made it home. But we knew
the pike had done it, though we watched

the council land the dribbling chassis
with a crane. We dared ourselves
back into the green water,

rafting down the overflow when it rained,
stooping under child-sized Niagaras,
leaping from the millstone-gritty walls.

I never saw a pike in the res
or in a keepnet and now I have one
in a dish, spit-roasted on a skewer,

I'm sorry for its cooked-blind eyes,
seared-off fins, flaking muscle.
I take it apart with chopsticks.

Frigidaire

There was plenty of danger at home
but we sought more in the bowels
of textile mills, reservoirs,
rubbish tips. Swings over dams
turned gallows or put us in traction.
Unleashed Alsatians coursed us from
building yards where we bathed in silos
of multi-coloured sands, sliced ankles
nimbling over Slinkies of razor wire.

"I dare you." I watch his muddy calves
shuffle into the maw of the derelict
fridge. His shoes catch its rubber lip
and sneer it back. I grab the chrome handle
and whump it shut. It takes hours
for the rocking to stop, the chilling appeals
to peter out. Who'd have thought the tattered
seal would give such suck? Now it's dark, and there's
battenburg and *Sing Something Simple* for tea.

Giallo

Soho. Reading a book on grief
and a cocktail menu. Long Island Baby
blows me a kiss sticky with vodka,

Malibu, orange and cranberry juice,
her thighs a mile of white sand, her rock pool eyes
swarming with the many-limbed creatures

of desire. I long to join her
till I remember that Long Island foams
with sharks and the bones of whalers,

bobs with the drowned buoys of bloated bathers.
The cocktail shaker racket brings me back
to this sugar-ringed table and Soho Square in the rain.

It's been two years, but when the barmaid sees
my watering eyes, I say "My father just died."
Not fair on her, but then your death

has made me mean and I change my order
to a Rusty Nail. She nods but it's clear
this is a new one on her.

She's all Baileys and crème de menthe,
milk and cherries. Would you have gone for her?
Philandering was your one and only optimism.

Crushed ice and the flash of chrome
slash back my midnight horrors of you.
Black gloves, flesh mask, felt fedora. You stalk

me down Italian lanes and Yorkshire snickets,
lurk in my bedroom, shoes under the curtain,
ready with razor, garrotte, ice pick.

Before I wake, you dig your skewers
into my brain, teasing apart the folds and lobes,
the carpaccio of flesh and memory until

only the cocktail list can keep you at bay.
Two or three more and then, *mio caro
assassino*, you'll be in the can.

Abductees

I've read their accounts and I sympathise
with those, in the night, in their homes, by surprise,
taken from children, husbands, or wives
and living in fear for the rest of their lives.

Who lose an hour here, an evening there,
barrelling home from God knows where,
who awoke doing seventy in the car
and found in the shower a tiny new scar.

Minuscule holes drilled into the molars,
polygonal bruising between the shoulders,
nosebleeds and blackouts and nightmares by day
and a pregnancy that just went away.

They never fetched me (although I prayed)
in their rainbow ships but I often strayed
to the brow of the moor where the stars were clear
and the crisp air crackled with something near

from so far away from that wintry town,
come to thaw the peat through and settle down
on Pole Moor or West Nab or on Holme Moss,
but no shadows joined mine upon the frost.

Goodbye Radio City

Forget the famous neon venue,
     New York is not a radio-friendly
          place. From the plane, a circuit board bristling

with transistors, capacitors, soldered
     avenues, the Empire State tracking
          across the green dial of Central Park,

fizzing through the channels of a hundred
     jabbering neighbourhoods. Nearer ground
          the radio waves smash and shatter

against concrete impedimenta.
     Snatches of song, Yankees games, *Nobody*
          Beats The Wiz! career and try to stay whole.

If radio thrives anywhere it's in
     cabs, cop cars, meat wagons, fire trucks,
          meshing the grid of lives, accidents

and catastrophes. But pictures dominate.
     The North Tower's mast only budded four
          radio transmitters, the rest TV.

Donald DiFranco, Steve Jacobson, William Steckman,
     Bob Pattison, Gerard Copolla, Isaias Rivera
          were tending their antennas that day,

enabling the city to watch, on cable,
     from satellite, their imminent closedown.
          Now there's a new rescue mission

out at Alpine, New Jersey, where
        Edwin Armstrong, father of static-free FM,
                stepped out of his 13th floor apartment

window in 1954.
        An overcrowded Empire State sees
                the transmitters leaving the island:

out of the centre, away from the heat,
        the dust, the fear. And anyway, everyone says
                you get the best views of the city from here.

London Whale

Two journeys you took in your last two days:
the first unwisely swimming west and then
carried unluckily east in a poor sling,
a small red watering can barely wetting
the wrongheaded brow that saw fit to squeeze
you through the gate line of the Thames Barrier.
Just another morning commuter
touching in or out with an Oyster card.
If you were heading for work, what strange job, this?
Unbriefed ambassador, curious key
to some ancient chamber flooded with guilt,
or love, or the rattling blades of that bad old trade
which it seems never touched you. Why here and now,
you smiling stranger? Do they sing about the bones
in the old museum? Did you *have* to chance it?
Look how sentimental you make me;
we're a city of visitors, you see.

Brighton Restored

Buckingham Road's solitary greengrocer
has let his shop go. Opposite our too-hasty
love nest, his window once shone
with pineapple, marrow, plantain and pumpkin
so pleased with themselves they might split.
Over twelve summers the window darkened,
thickening—an unrestored canvas—
from Matisse to Max Ernst. A wilderness
of overreaching bulbs, stray shoots,
liquefied tubers and greens. A thousand
generations of houseflies catacomb
the empty shelves.

I look back at our old double bedroom,
still curtained at noon. What rot has taken there?
What plates of unfinished takeaway
are stinking under the bed?
Are there piles of dress shoes gone to must
from the broken shower that blistered the walls?
Is another summer couple playing
at monogamy, choosing children's names,
calling psychiatrists out at dawn
to bring the foggy pills
that clouded my eyes and burned my skin
in winter sun?

I walk the route I used to run on nights
your eyes shone demon-bright in that room
so dark by day, too light at night for sleep.
Once, poisoned by paracetamol,
another time fleeing from your body
and the silken cicatrix where your "clumsy
African navel" bulged for the first five years
of your once-tropical life; the wound that spread
and mottled your torso with scarring
words of ancestral accusation;
and your fingers, ringed with African gold
from the "Prince" you fucked on your last trip home.

Becalmed by Palace Pier I wonder how
I let this drizzling town commandeer my twenties?
The West Pier, once reft, now pinioned
to the shore with steely new struts, no longer
speaks of gaps, of obliterated nights,
of a missing week in a hospital gown.
It is being restored. And maybe Alf's
Greengrocers will find a new lease:
reborn as a local estate agent,
Vespa dealer or Carphone Warehouse.
I know this: I won't be signing tariffs,
test driving scooters or viewing flats.
I'll be unmooring this town from its piers
and letting it drift.

Christmas at the School of Psychological Medicine

is a dish of Quality Street
with all the purple nut and caramels removed.
The drinks machine, like a seaside mayor,
stands stiffly in its tinsel regalia,
single teat dripping Kenco and Fanta.

What on earth am I doing here?
Portuguese men o' war float near the ceiling,
far from their spawning pools at Woolworths
and injection-moulded mistletoe
droops from the Saneline emergency number.

She's late. I sneak a piss in the Staff Only toilet,
return to the landslip of magazines:
nothing here newer than three years old.
We're not to be trusted with currency,
but *Top Gear* and *Celebrity Brides* can't hurt.

For the first time in weeks I may have something
to share, not just stare at her stylish boots,
the green pipes of her countrified corduroys,
before drifting off on the couch.
"Today, you let me see the baby you."

I dreamt in the hospital ward that my aunt
slid her hands inside my gown and pinched
a slub of flesh from my navel, spooled my gut
around her fingers, snapped it free
and dropped it in her knitting basket.

The holiday traffic is holding her up.
So leave a little earlier for God's sake.
Try taking the tube. I'm here and I'm the one
whose life is . . . better to grout my rage
with toffee between the molars. Chew it over.

Soloist

1

A new solo piece: first cornet, last post.
No theatre lights or hothouse tuition
to hoist me to the sacrificial C
high above my darling crotchets
that cleave to the foot of the stave.

You drank with the conductor and propelled me past
my peers, from third-cornet bit-part blower
to spotlit soloist, where I screeched and brayed
my *Onward Christian Soldiers*, marching as to war.

Caught on cassette for post-pub suppers,
the laughter climbing the stairs to my room.

2

The answer-phone tape filled up.
My sister twice, five times my mum,
an uncle, an aunt and then, at the last,
a new widow with it all to arrange.

3

On your big day you're quite the dandy.
Lying in state, more dapper than in life,
this crematorium chapel your Kremlin.

I once borrowed *Leninism Under Lenin*
with your library card to scare you,
to get back at you after you left,
and would stare impassively in your new flat,
before shutting the tome and reaching
for Einstein's *Principle of Relativity*.

Melomaniacal to a fault, you would *tut*,
continue to catalogue classical tapes.
Maybe Solzhenitsyn would do the trick
and make you feel blinkered, narrow, thick.

But there's a slide show of you in the States
I would beg to be shown as a boy.
A carousel-crumpled case in the loft,
hinging on stickers from your tour
with the Coldstream Guards—
Oklahoma, Albuquerque, Tallahassee,
Chicago, Seattle, Hawaii,
Dallas, Las Vegas, NYC—
before family, in the land of the free.

And when I made it to the Empire State,
I thought of you, skinny lad, gazing uptown,
world and euphonium at your feet
and the childhood burn on your cheek
the shape of Manhattan.

Desert Orchid

So much abduction, obituary and ossuary
that this long-jaw eye-roll flank-twitch
resignation gives me pause;
makes me long to lie amid the gamey straw
of a blameless life smoked out of nostrils flared
and into the paddock where souls strut,
on-the-muscle, unjockeyed, colourless.

Fitting

Traditionally, men will sit nearby in leather seats
or, in cheaper boutiques, on office surplus chairs.
Maybe flipping through *Men's Health* or *FHM*
while wives and girlfriends try things on, with dutiful assistants
pinning hems or sighing Saturday girls clattering hangers
back on racks, snarling with rolling eyes that "There's a queue."
But I pick my angle through the door of the changing room
to watch your naked feet rehearse the dance of sliding in and out
of pants and dresses, shoes and blouses, garments slipping up and down
with now and then a little show-and-tell as you yank the curtain,
reveal with a frown a tightly-waisted purple gown
then back again to just the feet, the turning ankles, balancing acts,
as you crane your neck to see how this or that looks from the back
and even if these things are chosen more with him in mind than me,
I'm held by your displays in proud and silent ecstasies.

Outlook Good

Another Kentuckian bourbon night's swill
and swell rocks me gently in the dark
as I wait for the nightly shipping forecast
while sailors in oils slick cross deck to hear
their fate from the oracle of Broadcasting House
and long to be cardiganed and coffeed
in Studio B with a black cab waiting
to drive the tarmac miles to sanctuary,
and a single helmsman paws over charts
by the light of a kerosene lamp that swings
and knocks his forehead with each restless turn
of the Atlantic as she takes more
and more duvet for herself and finally
kicks all the brackish green bedclothes to the floor,
and chilled by the six or seven rising
to gale force eight he sets his alarm for fifteen
minutes' time and tries to get his head down,
and wishes he were living in Switzerland
where shipping forecasts are as useful
as pollen warnings on the moon, but
I dream of casting off from the nodding
donkey derrick of Cape Cod with a bait-hold
jammed with slabs of frozen squid and forty miles
of monofilament, hooks, buoys, beepers,
leaders, gaffs and slime knives to dress the throngs
of swordfish I would haul on deck under
waxing moons that never wane in ocean
breaks that furnish forth fish like the pot
that wouldn't stop.

Luke Kennard

To a Wolf

I

When I wrote to the wolf my tie got stuck in the pillar box. I waved my arms and screamed, 'Who! Whooooo!'

In my more fanciful moments I LIKE TO IMAGINE A TINY MAN inside the pillar box and I LIKE TO IMAGINE HIM HOLDING ONTO MY TIE FOR 'DEAR LIFE' as I wave my arms and try to pull myself away from the pillar box which I imagine HE, for whatever reason, WANTS TO PULL MY FACE VERY CLOSE TO, PERHAPS IN ORDER TO SPIT IN IT.

I had to remove my tie to free my body from the pillar box.

Anyway, my letter was lost in the post and it was months before I heard from the wolf. Wounded, he assumed I had neglected him:

Dear Bastard,

Nobody came to see the great show in the arboretum, in spite of free tickets attached to balloons and let loose over the city. Let us take a moment to imagine that:

Nobody.

Balloons!

Yrs,

Wolf

Sometimes I just stand at the top of the tower and I look all over the city and I weep about it. (Although really I am weeping about something else).

II

'You can keep your opinions and your achievements,' avers the wolf. 'Keep also your *raison d'etres* and your holidays. What I like are *representations of myself.*'

The wolf is just crazy for representations of himself.

'Here's a picture of you, wolf.'

'Great!' cries the wolf.

'Here's a story about you.'

'Give it here!' cries the wolf.

The arboretum has grown over with scathing moss. Inside members of staff have been asked to remain calm while the flowers grow over their uniform and pin them to the glass wall. Twenty members of staff, boys and girls, and one enormous uniform—so as they look not unlike a monster with many heads and limbs.

'I was told, come spring, we would all drink lamb's milk,' mutters the concierge. 'But *now* look at us.'

I spend November building a zoetrope that depicts the wolf standing on his hind legs and chasing a hoop.

'That's the most beautiful thing I've ever seen!' the wolf exclaims.

We could all stand to learn something from the wolf.

'Hey!' yelps the wolf, later. 'This novel you wrote about me is rather circumlocutory. Where are all the descriptions of my *white-noise* fur and bloody breath like the steam from a kettle?'

'It isn't finished yet,' I snap.

III

Today was a good day, but it was not the best day. Not a pirate ship or a bottle of invisible ink or a conversation with your friend in Morse Code. No, there is a distinct lick of brass to the air which today is discreetly lacking.

A lovely job in a theatre! An ice rink in the square at night! Why should I be denied these things? (It is because I do not deserve them).

The wolf, staying now for the duration of winter, is capricious: 'I can't stand you any longer!' he hollers. Moments later he's taken me to town to buy me all of Chuck Palahniuk's novels. 'These are really good,' he says. 'You'll love this guy.'

My girlfriend and I agree that the wolf should pursue a career—and there is just the position for him at Whitehall:

WOLF REQUIRED, £20 per hour.

The wolf applies, commutes to his interview and, two days hence, is informed through the mail that, even in the face of gross competition, he has been given the post.

'Yipee!' he says—and sets off for Whitehall.

'So what does the job involve?' I ask, that night.

'Nothing,' says the wolf. 'As I understand it, they mean to pay me simply for being a wolf.'

IV

The Wolf and Religion: The wolf is Presbyterian.

'I don't know an awful lot about Calvinism,' he says, 'but as I see it, I'm *predestined* not to. I leave that sort of thing to the Lay Elders.'

'Does the Presbyterian church even *exist* anymore?' I ask. 'I thought they came up with it on a boat and it lasted the duration of the crossing.'

'No, that's Lutherism: after which he translated the bible into German, but was excommunicated by the Diet of Worms . . .'

'What's the Diet of Worms?'

'I don't know. Something to do with eating worms.'

'I'd look it up, but we used the encyclopaedia to make that raft last summer.'

'Yeah,' says the Wolf, 'that was a great Summer.'

~

The Wolf and his ailments: A progressively diminishing ability of the eye to focus.

My girlfriend takes milk and water down to the employees of the arboretum. As a symptom of dehydration and sleep-deprivation many of them now believe that they are Hydra—and challenge passers-by to lop off a head.

'Boy,' says the Wolf, leaning over my shoulder, 'you're like living proof that a little knowledge is a dangerous thing.'

V

Today the wolf is throwing sweets at me, scattershots of Dollymixture and chocolate covered peanuts.

'Look at this!' he says, furious. 'Press clippings from the future!'

He produces some yellowed scraps of paper:

> *The characterisation of the Wolf is brilliant. You can almost feel his breath on the back of your neck.'—The Tribune*

I feel the wolf's hot breath on the back of my neck.

'Read the next one.'

> *'I really like the bit where the wolf goes to prison.'—James, age 6*

'What's that about?' he demands. 'Am I going to prison?'

'These look more like press-clippings from the *past*,' I say. 'Probably a review of some other book about a wolf.'

The wolf is crestfallen. He coughs, he sits on his haunches. He stands up again.

'There are *other* wolves?'

'Not for me,' I pat him on the head, but it seems to grant scant comfort.

Plethoric Air

We all laughed at the decomposing clown,
But later shame sunk upon us
And we got smashed on the balcony.

I had lost my left shoe in the blood.
The doyenne and her ten attachés
Scattered blossom on the divans.

We were charmed by a famous puppy,
A dozen gold pins in her forehead;
A tendency to speak ill of the dead.

'The dead are so stupid,' she said.
An attaché took me by the temples and ordered,
'Look: that advertisement on the crevasse;

Notice the inverted commas around "*crazy adventures*"
Grow bigger than the words themselves,
Framing the very hills and the valleys.

Like that man by the fountain who changed his name to #:
But ask him *why* and he'll say,
"You've got to stand out from the crowd, right?"

And other redundant platitudes.
Disappointment kicks you like an ostrich:
Bloody, sandy and hard.

In other news, we grow weary and suspicious—
And we'll ask you to defend yourself
Using words we already hold to be meaningless.'

I lay back, bumping my head on the war.
Every solid object has been declared part of the war.
I saw the puppy flex her golden needles.

'You should talk to this guy,' I said, 'he's funny.'
'Talk to him?' she spat.
'I wouldn't even eat his brain.'

The Murderer

I take the murderer for coffee.
'Make sure you don't *murder* your coffee!'
I joke. He likes my jokes.

Later I swing a plank into his face:
This is to stop him enjoying himself—
Which is integral to the rehabilitation process.

His mouth trickles blood like a tap quarter-turned.
He likes my analogies. 'Hey, Murderer!'
I yell, '*Murdered* anyone recently?'

The murderer likes to play badminton.
When he loses, I say, 'That's what you get for being a murderer.'
When he wins, I say,

'I guess you got yourself in pretty good shape
Murdering all those people.'
I'm not about to let the murderer forget he's a murderer.

When I dance with the murderer I let him lead
Because he is the more proficient dancer—
'Just be careful not to murder me!' I tease.

The prison sits on the horizon like a great ash-tray—
When we travel I give him the window seat.
'Hey, murderer, would you like a sandwich?' I say,

[34]

'Or would you rather murder someone?'
The murderer eats his cheese and ham sandwich.
'The forecast is for snow,' I tell him.

II. PICNIC

The murderer has just had a haircut.
'Your new haircut makes you look like Judas,' I say.
That night we go to see a musical adaptation

Of the September 11th terrorist attacks.
It doesn't go down well—in fact the show
Is abandoned due to audience derision.

'Oh, I'm *sorry*,' cries the director.
'Is five years too soon for you people?'
The next day it is sunny, so we have a picnic

With French bread and olives and cheeses
And a box of wine. The breeze is cold.
'I think I will write a novel called:

My Picnic with a Murderer,' I say.
We stay out until the light is low and the grass is damp.
The murderer gets bitten by a red ant.

When we get home I dump the picnic basket
In the kitchen with the washing up and the half-eaten
Cans of beans. A half dead fly crawls up the window.

The murderer never cleans the house
Due to self-esteem issues.
He doesn't believe that he deserves a clean house:

He believes that the house should mirror his soul.
I take the murderer shopping for a new wardrobe.
'Let's get you spruced up,' I tell him.

I buy him a little sailor suit with *murderer* embroidered
On the collar. My mother's been calling again;
Somebody sold her a carpet she doesn't want.

III. THE DISGUSTING TELEPHONE

The murderer has written a libretto.
'It's not bad, for a murderer,' I tell him.
'Maybe you could round up some other murderers

And they can perform it for you.'
We do not mention the libretto again, even when
The murderer refuses to be interviewed

For *True Crime* magazine. 'I'd have thought
That was right up your street,' I say.
'You know—crime, and all that.'

I have a separate telephone for talking to the murderer.
I call it The Disgusting Telephone.
The murderer likes to keep abreast of current affairs.

'You'll be pleased to hear there's been a natural disaster,'
I tell him. 'Over seven hundred dead.
I expect that's made your day, hasn't it?'

Every Tuesday we visit the Job Centre.
'Unfortunately nobody currently requires a murderer,'
I report. 'Still. There's always next week.'

The murderer smiles, patiently. On his birthday
I take the murderer to the best restaurant in town.
'Don't you know any other murderers we can invite?'

I ask. He doesn't reply, so I don't push the point.
'Here's to you, murderer!' I raise my champagne glass.
I'm thinking of taking up Yoga or something.

IV. GIRLFRIEND

I pick up the murderer's girlfriend at the station.
'Have you travelled far?' I ask her.
'No,' she says. 'It should have been half an hour,

But a horse died on the tracks.
It took them three hours to remove it, poor creature.'
'A horse is rather like an unforgivable sin, isn't it?' I say.

She is wearing a dress made of shag-pile carpet;
She is drinking a can of orangeade.
She has another can of orangeade in her pocket.

'I can see you like orangeade,' I say,
'But what attracted you to the murderer?
Do you have some kind of a *thing* about murderers?'

She watches the raindrops on the passenger window.
'I hope *you're* not a murderer, too,' I say.
'One murderer in my life is quite enough for me.'

'Actually,' she says, quietly, 'I think we're *all* murderers.'
I brake for a red light. 'That's lucky,' I say.
'I imagine it would be difficult going out with a murderer

If you weren't a moral relativist.'
The murderer is watching a chat show and eating
His third tube of Oriental Spice flavour crisps.

His girlfriend gives him a can of orangeade.
He acknowledges her with a grunt.
'If you need me, I'll be checking my e-mails,' I say.

V. GOVERNMENT PAPER CONCERNING CARE FOR YOUR
   MURDERER

I am to be allocated a new murderer.
The conference takes place on a summer evening,
The undersides of seagulls illuminated by floodlights.

'God bless you, tiny flying cathedrals,' I mutter.
'You probably don't understand that, being a murderer,
But it's called a metaphor. It's a thing I use for talking about
      seagulls.'

I check-in the murderer with my coat.
The strip-lit foyer smells of sausage rolls,
Lined with posters for Renaissance art exhibitions

And unmanned tables selling audio-cassette interviews.
The notice boards hold more defunct announcements.
A bell rings and we climb the ladders to the auditorium.

I do not like my colleagues or their sweaters
Which appear to be decorated with an arcane form of sheet music.
Each time I look at their bellies or chests

I hear the antiphonal strains of ancient chants.
I do not like the speaker or the host;
Their boot-black hair and woollen bonhomie.

They say things like 'Watch this space!'
And 'Hold that thought!' when they are leaving
Temporarily to get a sandwich.

The murderers were left in a holding pen for reallocation,
Only someone forgot to lock the gate, so now they roam
The centre saying, 'How do you do?'

And 'I really enjoyed your talk.' I find my murderer sitting
Alone in the car park and I say, 'Come on murderer,
Let's go home.' Silently, he climbs into the passenger seat.

A Pergola of Exceptional Beauty

'That's the last time I have sex with a ghost,'
Declared Patrick, but the ghost knew better.

After four years failing to come up with a slogan
Patrick's focus group were sick and listless;

They lolled sideways in their chairs,
Stirring the same cups of tea for minutes on end.

'My notebook is digging into my stomach,'
One complained. 'It's too *cold* in here.'

After eight hours of that, Patrick was demoralised
And just about ready to have sex with the ghost again.

Despite various cultures warning that it damned you
Patrick placed his fingers on the ghost's back.

The ghost took Patrick to a pergola of exceptional beauty;
A tower block collapsed in his chest.

Gerald Variations

Maybe you have an empty room to charter to his likeness; but you do not know this Gerald by whom I am enthralled—because he renovates my mind with his very presence like a hardback anthology of insights I dip into whenever I am bedridden by a head-cold. And unfortunately asking him about it is out of the question.

Maybe you have a missing button that fell into the bouillabaisse; but you do not know this Gerald whom I cannot stand—for the esoteric arrogance of his every utterance is like a vital ritual in an obscure and terrifying religion. And unfortunately he is not here to defend himself.

Maybe you have exaggerated the dubious moral relativism of your township's museum; but you do not know this Gerald to whom I am indifferent—for his trespasses have come to disappoint me, like the overstated hallucinogenic properties of a harmless dried root. And unfortunately I have spent all the money intended for utility bills.

Maybe you have recorded an album with a caged seagull and two agnostic percussionists; but you do not know this Gerald whom I love—for I have known the fiscal security of his patronage like a doctor's hand against my heart. And unfortunately he will not extend the same courtesy to you.

Maybe you have manufactured and sold a range of oblivion-flavoured sweets; but you do not know this Gerald whom I loathe—for I have felt the humiliation of his scorn like fat spitting from a frying pan or fireworks in a celebration against me. And unfortunately I was too taken aback to retaliate.

Maybe you have had sex on a bicycle without sustaining or bestowing a single injury; but you do not know this Gerald with whom I am currently eating a hot dog—because we are both hungry. And unfortunately I have dripped mustard onto his copy of *The Cloud of Unknowing*.

Maybe you have sought his face in cross-sections of courgette; but you do not know this Gerald to whom I am currently dealing little deaths—because I trod in dog excrement on my way back from the post office. And unfortunately I am wearing shoes with an especially deep tread.

Maybe you have skipped across the rocks and broken your leg on an abandoned rowing boat; but you do not know this Gerald to whom I feel superior—as, for all his intelligence, he has forsaken his humility and humours my ideas like a cat toying with a shrew. And unfortunately the irony of the situation is lost on me.

The Dusty Era
for S.F.

One day he was walking behind her with several colleagues from the Embassy when the hairgrip fell out of her hair (bronze, decorated with three parrots) and clattered to the pavement. It was Stockholm, and high winter. She was deep in conversation with a girlfriend and didn't hear. His colleagues chuckled and continued to admire her legs.

They walked five blocks before she noticed her hair around her shoulders, patted the back of her head and stopped walking. She turned and looked first at the pavement and then up, where she caught his eye. She looked hurt, as if something in his face had apologised for conspiring against her with lesser men (he responded with an apologetic grimace) then she took her girlfriend's arm and walked on, hurriedly.

Two summers later, looking for cufflinks for the reception, he found the hairgrip in a pawn shop in Östersund. An event Grabes describes as, 'One of those overdetermined little moments that gradually conspired to snap his reason like a chicken bone and force him into organised religion, more credulous than even the altar boy.' (*ibid*, p. 136) It should be noted that Grabes was one of the men walking with him that winter evening in 1956, and that he was, in all probability, quite attracted to E. himself—a fact that throws Grabes's more spiteful observations into relief.

He stood with a hip-flask, complaining in the port, a parcel of Christmas presents under one arm. Each day contains a hundred subtle chasms. You can betray someone by not smiling, murder them by not saying 'Mm,' at the appropriate points in the conversation.

Years later he sat on the swingset in the playpark, an unopened letter from his daughter in his inside pocket. He was throwing pine-cones at the rusty ice-cream van. 'You should be banned from describing anyone,' he said out loud in the condensation. Two of his would-be future biographers crashed into each other on the autobahn and were killed instantly. One of them was me, hence my omniscience.

The Embassy was dustier after that—it came to be known as the Age of Dust or the Dusty Era. A fault on the line made the intercom pop sporadically like a man about to say something difficult.

The Last Days of Advertising

I. THE MIGRAINE HOTEL

It was one of those bashed-in silver nights;
A sense of work unfinished like an itch
In the very centre of your head.

H. sat in a cloud at the bar drinking
The stagnant English beer we hated,
His thoughts flicking away like shrimp.

Lead us not into television, was one of them.
He translated it into words and spoke it.
That night we heard him through the wall

Praying, 'God, I am nowhere. Or I am clawing
My way up a column of something fleshy—
I think it might be my own mouth.

I think I live in my own mouth. Please send money.'
We agreed: H. had become an empty signifier;
Although none of us could agree what that meant.

A registered trademark or a blimp or whatever.
Really, the end-credits approached all of us;
Our qualifications were not recognised

By the new administration—as if the cat
Walking over the board game was the context
And not, as we had thought, the boardgame.

'And we are just toppled pieces,' he murmured.
'Those nights we stayed up worrying we were frauds:
Now we may see them as our only real work—

The diagnosis of our own fraudulence.
Tell me,' he said, 'what is the German for:
I never even learned a second language?'

II. AS THE MENU IS TO FOOD

The sky was violently blue.
Never a good sleeper, H. had constructed
A paperclip mausoleum the size of his hotel room.
For breakfast he thought about fear,
How it underpins everything like toothache.
We awaited our arrest.

Further evidence of his brilliant downfall:
He has struck-through every line in his diaries
(1968–2008) and written, in the final margin,
Cliché. So where next in our sparkling
Hangover? To Tuesday, inexorably.
Each day an ocean with imagined liners.

This house H. imperfectly inhabited,
Dreaming every night of a former house.
H. sat on the place like a sticker,
Like a word misused for years,
Listened to the saws panting next door.
The mice are our footnotes.[1]

---

[1] [Squeak, scrabble-scrabble-scrabble, sounds of eating, etc.]

III. HIS LAST JOB WAS FOR COCA-COLA

The 30-second spot comprising a slow pan across a graveyard, and a bi-plane, skywriting, as the camera closes in on a gravestone inscribed simply, YOU, before focusing on a close-up of an abandoned can of Coke at the side of 'your' gravestone, spilled slightly over the ground, closer still to reveal an ant paddling with one foot at the surface of a brown droplet on a blade of grass before we pan out again to reveal the skywriter has written the following:

> *Coca-Cola predates you . . .*
> *. . . and will outlast you!*

Followed by a slow fade to the familiar cursive, this time not in skywriting, but superimposed over the scene in white:

> *And there is absolutely nothing*
> *you can do about it!*

H.'s original catch-phrase was over 17,000 words long, divided into chapters and concerned, among other things, our living 'outside of history' a state blamed by H. largely on Coca-Cola itself. One chapter entitled 'We Are History's Exoskeleton', which digresses on the theme of exoskeletons *per se* and the 'kingdoms of insects' about which we know 'Not nearly so much as we think we do, nor ever will.'

Like much of the tagline, this was considered excessive by the junior copy-editor who simply took the first and last sentences of the thesis and came up with the graveyard scenario by herself, which enraged H., (who refused to attend the awards ceremony at which the commercial was later honoured), but then so did everything at that point, enrage him.

Yet he recalls this time fondly in his autobiography.

IV. HE DOESN'T LOVE ANYWHERE ELSE, EITHER

The street is paved with human teeth,
Set in cement, like little white and yellow cobblestones—
Looks like a giant ivory snake.
The cottage is thatched with his own hair.
That's where H. lives and where all of his telescopes are.
It's such a terrible town people brag about having lived there:

'I saw a whole *group* of men smoking
Through their tracheotomy holes! A group!
Like it was a conference of tracheotomy-hole-smokers!'
And 'Here the babies push their *mothers* in prams!'
Which is presumably a crack about underage mothers.
But he lives there because he is authentic.

He doesn't love it, the town, like a monkey
Presumably doesn't *love* trees. Anyway,
How could you say you *loved* that place
Out of anything other than journalist-baiting bombast?
In no way, that's how. So he doesn't *love* the town,
But he stays because he doesn't love anywhere else, either.

Chris McCabe

Three London Poems

TREES AT HACKNEY WICK

black ventricled bare branches
child-angry scrawl on wax paper
plastercracked neutral chalk-white sun
softedged silhouettes through railings
up concrete steps to the overhead bridge
(*good morning london*) & look back—
trees have gone mad, branched up   up
trying to stop sky falling on them
blind-fanning locusts from their hair.
     (enters the drunk's
swinging giblet of spit stuck to the lip
handle of horror rolls in the cinemascope bus
      & everyone looks

PALIMPSEST

station's manual digital clock clacks
directs the scene: take   take   take
8:03:46   47   48   49   50

below district line's deliriously driven drinks' trolley
low black london orange-flecked
like hot scattered ash
reflection undissolves transparent
extinction's memories of the shallows—
silhouette woman unknown & alone:
I have been looking straight through you

JUBILEE LINE

pubic triangle of the nest in the branch bones
barbed wired white disc
tumbles unripe fruit from a ripped net
& window-lolls like a tongue of boiled ham.
thought   shocked-sleep
aerials parallaxed by lamp-light
three minutes & forty-eight seconds
polyester dreams
woke where east is the turned-out glove of west
                        & everywhere burnt silver

Poems for Lunch

1

penetrative genius lock-picks concentration's hub
BIG ISSUE shoved between eyes & poems
when last week the same man announced it
with a tune : di-derrida
which made no difference & with more patience
but the same lack of money   still don't buy it
Thames prickled silver like silverfoil pricked
for recreational drug use seen once high
stop at the booksellers to flick a guide to fishing
by a quartet of the best anglers from the 1960's
first turned page has a balding picture in black & white
with text I won't forget:
"fish are not concerned with your comfort only their own"
which makes me think of a smoking jacket, slippers
& a hot fish pie
& the Thames bereft of dead fish, even, on their side
only amoeba explosions of soft silt mud
which brings footsteps & time into the realm of the synchronised
up the steps   to the poetry factory

2

capsules (millenium wheel) float in front of the sun
& suck the heat out of me.
I didn't know glass could do that.
rafters of a park bench place to think
head back to the wall
crumbles like oat into my hair.
hour of the cover version.
back to inherited roots.
if the houses were to burn again
it would probably be too hot
but we could always take our trousers off.
correlative to the man with a ferret on a leash
always   there is only/so much possible.
the next thing on the hot glass of sleep
where the wheel is a bangle of alchemist's phials
see the 8 on a digital watch
& hope there is no numbered structure
to the ways I'll wake & try to speak.
one revolution & the lunch break's gone.

Michelangelo Manufactured by the Murdoch Empire

Michelangelo as well, duplicitous
with a half-eye for what you wanted
BBC docu-dramatizes with freedom of evidence
jesus-figure plays him, *asides* to camera
he too knew what sells
faker—*poseur*—forger—
of a 1000 year old Cupid
plastered, coated in bio-yoghurt
& excrement
then buried underground
for six weeks, dug up
fizzing with authenticity

parable of the artist
the back of the beast that catches light
a side, facet, that eunuchs myth
strikes brilliance billiard ball white
Bacchus, androgynous
back-to-back to non-kosher Cupid
staggering asexually
(*Rupert Murdoch quip in a series of 2,000:*
"a genius on fleet street is someone
who is still sober at 12 o'clock")
over-erotic to sell
stomach swollen feminine
balls stumped penis like old spectators
at a cancelled game
re-seeing kitsch now dinner is on the table
shaping again, & still Riario—
the richest & most powerful in Rome—
rejects, shamed goggling
smashed over the curtained wall's plush baize
art unclassifiable in the cardinal's backlog

poem uploads to the Murdoch version
with a sudden sharp hot stink of FOX
genius of synchronicity
against the typos of time misspent
sitting at stool a'la Leopold Bloom
not reading, but tying shoes
& onto collectivist Wapping
[those offended by the hot name should look away now]
& *The Sun* like Stalinist lightbulbs to peasants
"devils' eyes"
suddenly milling for the country
I wonder why—says the non-believer—
what made them career a   yes
Post-Hillsborough
[look back now]

"SOMETHING IS ROTTEN IN THE STATE OF MURDOCH"
global pages veined marble
quarry building quarry
retro Cupid sells still
but Bacchus, bollockless
found backpaged & reproduced
in today's BETTERWARE catalogue

The Mananger
after The Brothers Karamazov

Dolphins are the Osmonds of the sea
the Mananger said & introduced his sons:
Benneth, Billip, Barreth & Whillip.
During the Summer they support Sunderland
and in Winter, Arsenal. It was October
so their bannered scarves said Arseland.

They had travelled to this festival to watch
Jack Clown & the Whites: the quietest
karaoke in town. Whillip asks for an oyster
and ends with a clam in his palm. Look,
there, in the moo-tent, he mutters—an upturned
motherfucker of pink & yellow udder.

Barreth is first to become romantically attached
despite being only seventeen with a comb-over,
he attracts interest as he puts forward his theory
on an unknown species capable of the Pregnant
Foetus. Disgusting, says Mananger: wash your
vowelly mouth out with consonants.

Benneth & Billip sit themselves under a tree
and look up—the first carousel they ever
knew has a whoosh in the trees—it swirls
childhoods of pink & purple paisley.

Whillip thinks: my brothers will be made to pay for this.

Abu Ghraib

the body as grave

the body as witchhunt

the body as gym locker

the body as bodybag

the body as bacteria

the body as escape route

the body as borrowed

the body as business

the body as dim sum

the body as wham-bam thank you mam

the body as beggar

the body as banquet

the body as endgame

the body as bed-in

the body as dogbait

the body as batman

the body as party game

the body as blackmail

the body as 'the bitch in the box'

the body as bedwetter

the body as barbarbarbarbarbaranization

the body as inkblot

the body not as *what if*

      but what's done to it

The Pete Doherty in Prison Poem

Eyes panda-blacked from a ten year boozecruise.
Shelled & contused—which is *done-in* to you.

One clean day back when, took a picnic to a park in a place
called Tuebrook & etched immortal *Doherty* into the bark.

No protests to your latest arrest, caught in the chunk-
cheeked duck walk from Dalston to Shoreditch.

New media of mad nerd dementia. They need you
less than this post-vampyric need not to need them.

On the inside it's all stewing beef & pig kidney,
diced ox-heart with milk instead of cereal.

To miss the oaty warmth of Mother Time.
The dinner warden said he's got some reduced fish

for lunch, you said that must be tadpole soup
and not one stern face in the queue laughed or lapped it up.

You could blag your blogspot & still no one would care
who you were, bar the one you said you love who stares

from their brick walls on a catwalk to catcalls & dogsnarls.
This diary you've done no less urgent than Gramsci's

if more flippant &—as you would say—mostly pants from
        flap-to-flap.
You can flick back to what you've done then wrap it up.

Head shilly-shallies like a shambolic bambino. Tomorrow,
back to some onion argy-bargy along Brick Lane

then gigs in Glasgow. Total stretch: thirteen days.

Letter to Apollinaire Written in Père-Lachaise Cemetery

An Aubrey Beardsley designed France Télécom phonebox
Roof collapsed & nettled with cobwebs
We couldn't find you Guillaume
It rained so heavy
Last night I dreamt of killer monkeys with clowns' noses
Francis Picabia, Cendrars, Picasso
Playing poker on your tombstone
But found instead this Modernist Needle
And Jacqueline alongside you
(you should see Barry's b-sides, they're right up there)
We put a crapaud in your croci
Then went to find Jim
You can take a taxi to any tomb you want to see
Just say Avenue Circulaire or Number 63
It is only a baker's dozen to your centenary
The girl who loved poetry on the train at Nice in 1915
Who wasn't sure, but thought she might have heard your name
Now everyone knows who you are
You are going nowhere
Guillaume I too found love,
She makes a slip of the tongue, says 'smile' instead of 'stone'
Then showed surprised that a cemetery should have a W.C.
The living still need to go, some dead choose not to
We kissed at Colette & thought so much more at Abelard
Even here, men look down her blouse
Like Mummy might be lost there
Guillaume, it is only September & already on St Germaine
The windows show silver mannequins in winter wear
Conkers fall on stone like wooden knobs on bank doors
I want a tap on mine to keep me topped up
Such sweet tight release of a rosé cork
Cut a picture of the lost lovers in the death bibliothèque
But when she went to smell the drains again
I sat with two glasses & looked destitute
She knew where I was by virtue of Balzac's bust

I smiled as she strode back along the stones
Three wild cats passed along her path
There was no misfortune in that
As we waited for the grave of Jim to clear
A policeman shouted 'non alcools'
And marched us upright to the gates
And I've just turned twenty-eight
Next year we are coming to live here
And together give out guided tours
Starting 'each man kills the thing he loves'
(before you let rip you have to reign them in)
Charged at three euros a head or a bottle of vin

11 SEPTEMBER 2005

The Transmidland Liverpool to London Express
sonnets in simultaneous time

THE DIVIDE

North/South divide condensed to a taxi ride.
Her problems started long before renting a property
from a company called Total Masters, when she looks
in the pram & sings to the red scrunchie
of her baby's face: 'Walkies! Walkies!'
We got locked out from the lock-in & looked
through the door: how content they sat in the
subterfuge dark as each emptied out their glass.
Action fuckin Jackson & Orson Frickin Welles.
The world seemed to turn like a ball of foil on a
rubber glove. Green stalks uncontrolled outside
the bay windows—not weeds though, wildflowers—
that moved like stolen socks inside a lair & not once
did the barman call 'Lasts!' on those who stayed behind there

BATTERSEA

In the backdrop Battersea powershop, we took snaps
at 2:23 in the morning; Albert Bridge lit tenderly pink—
imagine the shame of being mugged there she said.
Every cabbie has a price to Dagenham, squat & check
as a prison dad, he talks Secret London as we go.
All-Ackroyd, sans-Sinclair. She sleeps on the black
backseat & dreams of fish to sing her further asleep:
Jackanory's John Dories. Other Dreams: painted gloves
in toby jugs. ATMs around Westminster were down,
nada nodes, an off-chance as politicians *depend* on them.
Maggie apparently named 'Daggers' as two from Barking
(there was no dog just the genesis of the Madhouse).
This is the only time you become defensive of the place
at three before dawn & for one sec blink: think it's yours

LIVERPOOL

They will be there with the same accent as me
I heard them where my body was, as I set up the balls
they spoke through a tannoy on a ride
called *Descartes' Bumper Cars*
then played three straight frames (I smiled towards them)
thirty-five red-green repetitions of aphorisms
the dull ivory click of balls—a stonehenge of the moment—
local words like poker in the fingers
being a veneer, a potential bluff, a set of rules
it's all available said the radio in 'L-L-L-L-L-Liverpool'
I thought of how the most vibrant boy at school
lived in the oldest house, mock-Tudor
and for the first time, maytime metropolis, that life-belt to me
did not diminish to what they want it to be: circuit-training
      in a cemetery

JUBILEE GARDENS

Clients in purple shirts stride across Jubilee Gardens.
There is grass & office space & constant movement.
Bitter snatches of orange rinds, leftovers of foxes.
Oak telephone pole like a trunk in the tree-branches,
bastard uncle plotting by phone in the next room.
I can't reach the Big Window & if I could, it would rain.
When we were on the bus there was a digital screen
that we watched as it said COMING SOON ... & then
showed us sitting, watching the screen, our stop now behind us.
It costs less to live East as the open season of culture ends
at Bromley-by-Bow. You know, it is typical of you
to talk to girls in your dreams about weight loss
and then to walk away—in your own fucking dream—
and not commission Uncle Joe to show them the door

DOCKLANDS

The DLR just goes round he said, a coast
route rail at a cut-throat rate. Each dock
smashed from beneath with a spotlight.
A pub called *The Artful Dodger* where people
go when the poetry workshops close.
Where glass browns to brick, this is where
the pod people live. Back to Dickens,
if you can live like this. Shadowed nets catch
and hold the words in the book you offer, you hold.
John Peel is dead. MacSweeney is dead.
Ivor Cutler has died. Clouds break & scan tripods
of light, a God Postcard, over HSBC & Canary
Wharf. Like He can honestly say this is New Babel
without a mutter, a slur, an iota of babble

THE HOME OF HUMOUR

The distance bus sparks red & blue,
the morning's kingfisher. When the
gales set in one careless word turns
the alleyway baby's bones to a delicious
chicken carcass. Liverpool turns history
to mythology before the country's disbelief,
next day all chickens come with free *Lemsip*
and handkerchief. Civilisation is when we stop
you don't understand, begin to laugh
at ourselves, not just each other. Have we made
laughter so much of who we are for so long,
we cannot dream we are culpable too?
Punchbag shadow swings in the stand-up tomb.
In Bar Retribution, brandy bleeds clotted cream

EUROSTAR

My brother stands by the Eurostar terminus & speaks
into his phone: 'I'm by some huge blue scaffolding'.
Termini as a pass-through place as travel makes of land.
So with poetry: to get *you* from one understanding
of experience to another, in the quickest possible time.
We laughed at the one that ended *written on the Silver
link, Euston to Watford, First of April 2004 at 11.26.*
As the trolley passed that poet took no shortbread,
opted instead to make *silverlink* in ink matter so much.
Did the cabinet of the cannon shift a bee's wing at least?
My brother's there still—I'll leave him for now, to wait.
Anyway, if he takes the wrong train he's lived on enough
rundown estates to have a piece of Paris-appreciation in him.
His mealtime best is *trois fromage* Findus Crispy Pancakes

THE PIER HEAD

Made the mistake of asking how her weekend went
then a twenty-five minute tirade on neolithic stones
and pagan churches, before my Monday Morning
Dialogue Box had even closed. How we all differ,
even as children: my love's world broke at her
brother's flare of the nostrils, I had to attach
a doll's head to a model plastic kangaroo.
I try to text 'love' & fumble out 'lout'.
Of course in Liverpool we are all employed
in the same open plan office, travel to work
by ferry & go on strike whenever the water
machine goes to pot. Honest we do, Mister Man
with the mortgage muscle. When I return to my
brought-up home, spiders spiral the gate's old chrome

BANKSIDE

Fed up with being cut-up by fat pedestrians
the only salvation is to people-watch.
Wisdom of Thameside orbs, moons locked
in asylum headclamps. Just to listen though
like a forensic anthropologist takes a skull
found on the *Mary Rose* & says it is so exciting
to touch the actual *people*. Stop swearing
in front of the fucking baby she said, he said I'm not
swearing in front of the fucking baby. Thomas-a-Kempis
too sanctimonious, at least St. Augustine buttered
his own dirt. Feeling Churchillian she said Horace said
'poets create monsters' yes though but what about God —
and anyway *you* you're too ugly to be written in.
Now please pass me the fucking desert menu

ISLINGTON

Islington's congregations of bar pimps makes him think:
why do porno stars grow pony tails?
It takes the stud motif a little too far.
To be a libertine in your twenties is to wear a flatcap it seems.
Hope lifts us up, the Anchor of ever-after weighs us down.
I love you, you do know that don't you?
These discoveries on your generation worries though,
it is like finding a swinging brick for a heart
in the simple process of a skin graph.
Keep breathing boys! How they had to break off the branches
and root them in wires to become the rustic band of ecology
immerse yourself in greenery become part of the scenery
when the barman came to clean up after us
he asked if this pint was dead: I said no, it's working on me

HIGHTOWN

In a dark dark town there was a dark
dark street. Down the dark dark street
there was a dark dark pub. In the dark
dark pub there was a dark dark shelf.
On the dark dark shelf there was a book
called *Competition & Monopoly*. Reproduction
mustachioed Mona Lisa splattered with the
house gravy. We took an axe to the
Constitution Club. Say cheers with a Guinness
sounds like a marble medley of black
snooker balls. Twelve the maximum.
Take this cover-up on a city with issues:
Mr Thornton with his strap-on choc cock.
In a dark dark town there was a dark dark

A QUICK SURVEY

There are landladies that went senile thirty years
ago, rents have not increased since the Women's March.
The people who live in her rooms think it's political
—it is the only thing they have in common—
and pull together to co-operate under the tag of *commune*.
Does this sound like you? Well good luck to you
I think I think your luck is good. We lived in Wild West
Ham for seven months & the rent that we paid was more
than the wage we made. Does this sound like you?
If your answer is Yes to either of these then please
make the time to complete the attached ticklist.
If you are *other* do you think it matters? It is an
atypical Tuesday in October, at Waterloo Station
tampons are trampled in the wet tarmacadam

BIRKENHEAD

Another place, of another select language
imagine how untrue it is—London news drips into bowlers—
then the pretension of intelligence despite accent:
did I say *Catullus* I meant *calculus*?
Back in liverpool we allowed 'ovale' to be scrabbled in
which wasn't in the Collins Dictionary Colin held
—three distinct definitions around a hole—
soft vortices of the Mersey on the tourist route
past a smokable clock (Little Bill stuck 20 to 6)
untelevised dock warehouses, beetle-humped rubble (a.k.a. Bootle)
cut silk of seagulls over the Bank Holiday pub's sporan-latched yard
opened to Victorian park, desolate we laughed
towards the friable background of doubles-bars
and the louche music of money pockets, expectant mothers

STEPNEY GREEN

From the moment we arrived we talked only of leaving
and as we prepared to go, decided to stay.
Doorman slumped like Frankenstein's dream of winter coal.
An ATM had replaced the DJ's decks.
You took a call on the phone from a Mrs Tyne
first named Phyllis, thick-lensed hub of a Bud
is a centre at least of what this is: drowned sun
stickled with lost molten stars.
I will drink only from the most masculine of straws.
Pinhead of a barboy in an oversized shirt.
Teeth stained from reincarnation
on the television screen above, he exercises cheekbones
though wastes boyscout ears only to talk & reassure:
if this is truth, the elephant of tomorrow dumps into an eggcup

ROMFORD

In the bus bay starlings risked wing & claw
for a jawful of shortcrust crumbs. One must
have spread the worm: sky swarmed & chipped
into black pips. I was kind of with it but just not
quite, having ironed my combats before leaving
the house. Sex is natural she said or why would
there be condom machines in the cubicles?
Romford just out-of-the-loop: no Olympiad,
only control-freak. Then consider this new
urban sport: dismantling the market stall
before the town paints red the dead fish
left on wet slabs. This is the only time we find
to nail it down—you're in town & we get to talk:
I become King of Clubs still not scared by killer clowns

MUSWELL HILL

No taxis in Toy Town. The rank
is a silver shelter that rings on silence.
We could have walked to the Church Pub.
No arseholes with aerosols. At East Finchley
tube lies McDonalds HQ, the Uni of Ronnie Mac.
What punnets of protein do the staff down in the canteen?
Outside the venue a bush-rustle, the wrestle with the rest for the bus.
W3 to Wood Green. Blue-veined tube cuts through Islington,
disconnected & in need of the light of The Angel.
The great rush-through East begins.
And the band? We could have had
it so much better. We could have
had it so. We could have.
We.

MERSEYBUS

The thing is Janine, when I wear my husband's
dressing gown I strangely don't feel like a man—
I feel like a woman in a grown man's dressing gown.
I mean, it's at least half his life isn't it?
Do you think we could add two letters to the alpha
bet & nobody would notice? Bet a laugh we could.
Her hair's like a split golf ball & her head the wood
to hit it with. What he does is this: takes his whiskey
into the wild woods only to have words & curse
his dead dad. Did I tell you Dolly's going to New York?
The thing is, if you can smell the bacteria you can
actually *see* bad breath. I tell you: it's the place
itself I'm thinking with half the time, and it's closer
to a pair of drainpipes than any actual paradise

BRIXTON

I diverse, she says, though she means *digress*,
and closes the line in time for Pete Waterman
to order Charles Saatchi off his Southbank estate.
At the Tate you cannot dissolve sugar cubes
through mere contemplation alone. Doherty's
the golden boy at the Brixton Academy—
spot the scabs between the clothing gaps.
A vampyre has bit his wrists, but where Johnny Rotten
put a curse to cut the media's purse, the doe-eyed
junky comes out in daylight to strings of hotdogs
and dipped breadsticks. He crawls from the back
of vans with gnarled cans, and though his backstage
rider is not with bats, he approaches his fans
from the back, lit with candles & limegreen absinthe

West to Central

It is Christmas when Starbucks give red cups
at no extra cost. People tired but happy in the
other dream itinerary. Sleep-deprived babies.
Plastic maps fragile in top pockets. Every day
in West London, no word of a lie, Jools Holland
hops onto the tube in time to a boogie-woogie
backbeat. By the time he gets into your television
he introduces his next act as *Berk Rattatat*. Which
Googles at ninety-three hits. Typos or sub-cult?
In a well-known art gallery the rape of Baghdad
is played-off against a pastiche of porn. A critic says:
'the pillage plagues me, the porn will please me,
the connexion between the two falls flat.'
In W.C. my hands know what my eyes have seen

The Rapies

is what I read, looking quick
in the physical self-help section
at every cure-all under the *Sunday Sun*,
His Dark Materials sold as a loss leader
like underwater swimming reaching coloured
plastic fish for air, it occurred
at the dada chequerboard game
of the checkout how strange it was
that *we* took everything out, put it back
—then paid—rain cracked the taxi windscreen
like Pollock's frozen thought of bankruptcy,
in the rearview a darkened microfiche of my face
beginning to transfer to the other side
like a spent, fuggy hologram

BARKING

Kicking out time at the *Barking Dog*.
Bodies, doors, arches, trees. To travel
and arrive here. Creatures of culture
like dwarves in a cornfield. Six hours
south by coach, tube, bus—semantic
branches break & bleed carnival to LCD.
If desperation can celebrate put taxis on
the ticklist this Friday. Placebo
of the all-night margarita specialist.
I like wine with an amnesiac finish
that bites when it's too late to take back.
Midnight reality: a bowling ball through
the Fairy Tale rehearsal. No strike optional.
Cabbies frown at size 48 font. Stare at their bodies.

DOVECOT, LIVERPOOL

Relationships (all possibilities from one self
journeys all the *ways* out to each of us)
we run for the red bus not knowing its number
it is fun how your body's contortions pull faces
                              beneath your clothes,
we watch the sound of the siren to recognize the service—
is this ours, I mean, can we do ourselves in by the way we feel?
The cup of the city spills, shatters—it is called perspective
                              it is everywhere—
the way the tip of a cigarette in the dark could be a light on a ship
I found you, the only one to keep my fact file warm amidst the bricks
no cop, I should say, could *police* our language in any crowd,
two cogs bit in to the code called love, in a system
                              only we could hack into

[73]

Lightning Source UK Ltd.
Milton Keynes UK
06 May 2010

153797UK00001B/22/P